MW01000199

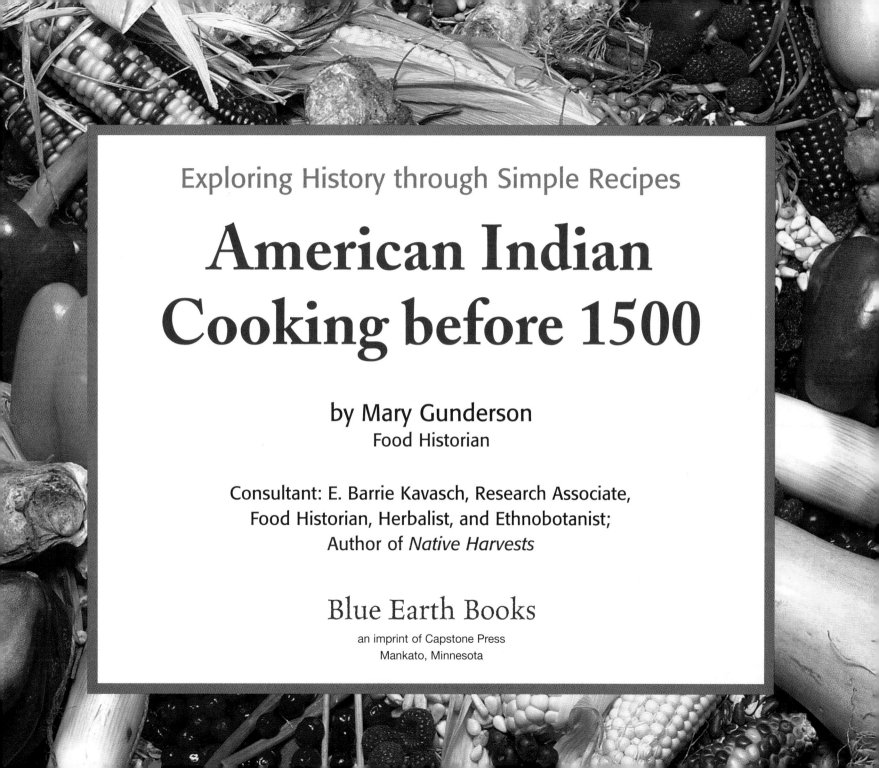

Exploring History through Simple Recipes

American Indian Cooking before 1500

by Mary Gunderson
Food Historian

Consultant: E. Barrie Kavasch, Research Associate,
Food Historian, Herbalist, and Ethnobotanist;
Author of *Native Harvests*

Blue Earth Books

an imprint of Capstone Press
Mankato, Minnesota

Blue Earth Books are published by Capstone Press
151 Good Counsel Drive, P.O. Box 669, Mankato, Minnesota 56002
http://www.capstone-press.com

Library of Congress Cataloging-in-Publication Data
Gunderson, Mary.
   American Indian Cooking before 1500 / by Mary Gunderson.
      p. cm.—(Exploring history through simple recipes)
   Includes bibliographical references (p. 30) and index.
   ISBN 0-7368-0605-9
   1. Indians of North America—Food—Juvenile literature. 2. Indian cookery—North America—Juvenile literature. 3. Indians of North America—Social life and customs—Juvenile literature. [1. Indians of North America—Food. 2. Indian cookery. 3. Indians of North America—Social life and customs.] I. Title II. Series.

E98.F7.G85 2001   ✓ j 970.00497
394.1'08997—dc21   G   00-036829

Summary: Discusses the everyday life, cooking methods, common foods, and hardships and celebrations of American Indians before 1500. Includes recipes.

Editorial Credits
Editor, Rachel Koestler; cover designer, Steve Christensen; cover production and interior designer, Heather Kindseth; illustrator, Linda Clavel; photo researcher, Katy Kudela

Acknowledgments
Blue Earth Books thanks Mike Scullin, Professor of Anthropology, Minnesota State University, Mankato, for his assistance with this book.

Photo Credits
American Museum of Natural History, cover, 13 (bottom), 18 (right top), 18 (right bottom); Gregg Andersen, cover (background), 11, 13 (top), 21, 25, 29; North Wind Picture Archives, 8, 10, 14, 17, 18 (left), 20, 22, 23, 26, 28; Mike Scullin, 24 (all); Cahokia Mounds State Historical Site, 9; University of Washington, 12; Library of Congress, 16

Editor's note
Adult supervision may be needed for some recipes in this book. All recipes have been tested. Although based on historical foods, recipes have been modernized and simplified for today's young cooks.

1 2 3 4 5 6 06 05 04 03 02 01

Contents

Cooking Help

Recipes

References

Metric Conversion Guide

U.S.	Canada
¼ teaspoon	1 mL
½ teaspoon	2 mL
1 teaspoon	5 mL
1 tablespoon	15 mL
¼ cup	50 mL
⅓ cup	75 mL
½ cup	125 mL
⅔ cup	150 mL
¾ cup	175 mL
1 cup	250 mL
1 quart	1 liter
1 ounce	30 grams
2 ounces	55 grams
4 ounces	85 grams
½ pound	225 grams
1 pound	455 grams

Fahrenheit	Celsius
325 degrees	160 degrees
350 degrees	180 degrees
375 degrees	190 degrees
400 degrees	200 degrees
425 degrees	220 degrees

Kitchen Safety

1. Make sure your hair and clothes will not be in the way while you are cooking.

2. Keep a fire extinguisher in the kitchen. Never put water on a grease fire.

3. Wash your hands with soap before you start to cook. Wash your hands with soap again after you handle meat or poultry.

4. Ask an adult for help with sharp knives, the stove, the oven, and all electrical appliances.

5. Turn handles of pots and pans to the middle of the stove. A person walking by could run into handles that stick out toward the room.

6. Use dry pot holders to take dishes out of the oven.

7. Wash all fruits and vegetables.

8. Always use a clean cutting board. Wash the cutting board thoroughly after cutting meat or poultry.

9. Wipe up spills immediately.

10. Store leftovers properly. Do not leave leftovers out at room temperature for more than two hours.

Cooking Equipment

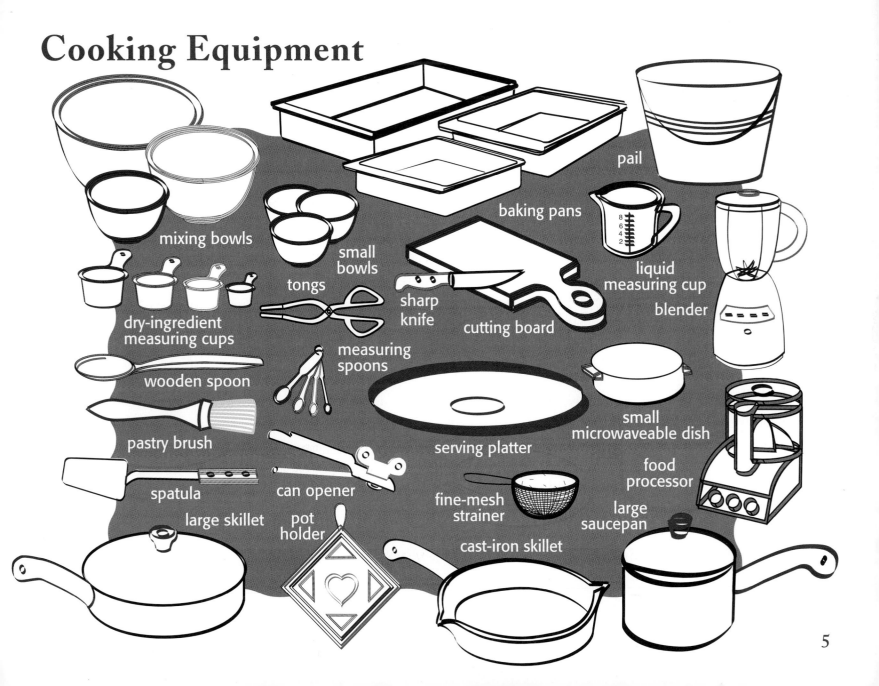

mixing bowls

baking pans

pail

small bowls

tongs

dry-ingredient measuring cups

sharp knife

cutting board

liquid measuring cup

blender

measuring spoons

wooden spoon

serving platter

small microwaveable dish

pastry brush

food processor

spatula

can opener

fine-mesh strainer

large saucepan

large skillet

pot holder

cast-iron skillet

5

The American Indians before 1500

Between 500 and 1000 years ago, thousands of American Indian groups lived in North America. Some of these tribes were nomadic. They traveled in search of food, often moving to different locations each season. Other American Indian groups lived in areas with fertile soil. They built villages and farmed the land.

Each group passed its history and way of life from generation to generation. Older members told stories about the past and taught children about the group's traditions. They also passed on the tribe's ways of hunting, farming, and cooking.

The foods American Indians ate depended on where they lived. Groups who lived along the coast in the Arctic, Pacific Northwest, and California regions fished the ocean and rivers and hunted sea animals such as seals and walruses. American Indians in the Plateau and Great Basin were hunters, gatherers, and fishers. Many tribes in the Northeast and Southeast regions were hunters, farmers, and fishers. Southwest and Great Plains tribes hunted and gathered wild foods. Some planted large gardens. American Indians in each of these regions worked hard to make the most of their resources.

In each region, American Indians had times of plenty and times when they struggled to survive. American Indians celebrated successful hunts and had festivals of thanksgiving to honor a good harvest. They held special ceremonies to offer thanks to the earth for the plants gathered, the crops harvested, and the animals hunted. American Indians also experienced droughts, floods, and fierce storms that destroyed crops and killed wild game. During periods of drought, food was scarce. Many groups moved to different locations in search of food.

North America can be divided into geographical regions. The climates of these regions vary. American Indians who lived in each region ate foods that the climate supported.

Hudson
Bay

ARCTIC

Haida ○
PACIFIC
NORTHWEST

PLATEAU

Pacific
Ocean

GREAT PLAINS

Shoshone ○

Hidatsa ○

Iroquois ○

GREAT BASIN

NORTHEAST

Chumash ○
CALIFORNIA

○ Hopi

Cherokee ○
SOUTHEAST

Atlantic
Ocean

SOUTHWEST

Gulf of Mexico

7

Most American Indians planted gardens of corn, beans, and squash. They called these vegetables the Three Sisters.

Over time, American Indians formed trading networks that stretched across the North American continent. American Indians traded furs, tools, shells, turquoise, pipestone, flint, and copper. They exchanged information, news, and ideas. These routes allowed some groups to obtain a variety of foods. American Indians sometimes traded wild rice and seeds of fruits, vegetables, and herbs.

In the 1500s, European explorers arrived in North America. They were introduced to new foods and other American Indian goods. These foods soon made their way back to Europe. Some European explorers came to North America to conquer native groups and take them to Europe as slaves. American Indians' encounters with Europeans brought diseases to the tribes. They were not immune to illnesses such as smallpox and measles, which quickly spread from tribe to tribe. By the 1600s, many North American Indians began to die of European diseases and settlement conflicts. Today, American Indian groups that survived work to preserve their heritage through festivals, powwows, artwork, crafts, and other traditions.

The City of Cahokia

Much of the written information about American Indians before 1500 comes from archeological discoveries. Archeologists can learn a great deal about an American Indian group's daily activities, lifestyle, and culture from a historic site. One of the greatest American Indian discoveries was the city of Cahokia, near St. Louis, Missouri. This large settlement of possibly 25,000 inhabitants thrived from 1050 to 1250.

The Cahokians were both technologically and socially complex. They created an organized government and a trained work force. They fashioned hoes by attaching a stone blade to a handle. Members of the community established trade routes to the eastern coast and south to the Gulf of Mexico. Cahokian structures resembled those of Mexican cultures. These building designs suggest that the Cahokians had contacts far to the south.

The Arctic: Land of the Inuit Hunters

Inuit lived in the arctic region of the far north. Cold weather prohibited these native people from planting crops. They hunted walruses and seals as their main source of food. Inuit also fished year-round.

Inuit had complex methods for hunting seals. Seal hunting required a group of hunters to wait in perfect silence beside a seal's breathing hole. Within the hole, the hunter placed a feather or strung a thin slice of bone. When a seal arrived at the hole to breathe, the bone or feather jiggled enough to alert the hunter. The hunter thrust his harpoon into the hole. An Inuit hunter then cut away the ice around the breathing hole and pulled the harpooned seal onto the ice.

During winter months, most Inuit families lived in igloos. These dome-shaped houses made from snow blocks protected the Inuit from chilling winds. In the summer, the Inuit built sod houses, using whale bones as a frame. Some Inuit families constructed cone-shaped tepees covered with bear or caribou hides.

Trees did not grow along the Arctic coastline, so Inuit saved mattak to use as fuel. This layer of whale fat could be boiled into oil. The Inuit depended on mattak to heat and light their homes. For this reason, they did not use mattak to cook their food. They ate most meat raw or partially frozen.

Inuit who lived farther inland often hunted caribou. Inuit women dried caribou meat to save for times when food was scarce. They often stored meat on platforms built in trees to kept bears from stealing it. Women made caribou hides into clothing. During caribou hunts, women and children sometimes searched for blueberries and bearberries. These berries were a tart and welcome addition to their meals.

Snow Cream with Raspberries

Ingredients
8 cups fresh snow or
  8 cups crushed ice*
½ cup powdered sugar
2 cups fresh or frozen
  raspberries, partially thawed

Equipment
8 serving bowls
1-gallon (3.8-liter) pail or
  large bowl
dry-ingredient
  measuring cups
small bowl
measuring spoons
fine-mesh strainer

1. Chill 8 serving bowls.
2. Fill pail or large bowl with fresh snow, or prepare crushed ice.
3. Put ½ cup powdered sugar into small bowl.
4. Scoop 1 cup of ice or snow into each chilled serving dish.
5. Hold strainer over one dish of snow or ice. Sprinkle one tablespoon of powdered sugar through the strainer, shaking the sugar through until it is evenly spread over the snow or ice. Repeat with other dishes.
6. Spoon ¼ cup raspberries over each serving. Serve immediately.

*To make crushed ice
1. Freeze 4 trays of ice cubes if you do not have store-bought ice.
2. Place 16 ice cubes in blender.
3. Mix at low speed.
4. Put crushed ice in bowl and place bowl into freezer.
5. Repeat 3 times. Makes about 8 cups crushed ice.

Makes 8 servings

Inuit traveled by dogsled. They needed from two to eight dogs to pull a sled, depending on the load. Dogsleds carried loads of fish, furs, meat, and ivory. Most families needed at least 100 pounds (45 kilograms) of fish a day just to feed their dogs.

The Pacific Northwest: Haida Fishers

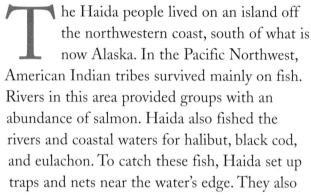

The Haida people lived on an island off the northwestern coast, south of what is now Alaska. In the Pacific Northwest, American Indian tribes survived mainly on fish. Rivers in this area provided groups with an abundance of salmon. Haida also fished the rivers and coastal waters for halibut, black cod, and eulachon. To catch these fish, Haida set up traps and nets near the water's edge. They also fished from canoes using unbarbed fishing hooks made from bone.

Before cooking, Haida pressed fish between rocks or blocks of wood to extract the oil. Eulachon, an oily fish, provided Haida with a good amount of oil. Some of this oil was poured into storage boxes to preserve fish. The Haida also served eulachon oil with their meals. They flavored bites of fish by dipping them in the oil.

Because Haida could catch salmon almost year-round, they often ate this fish fresh. The Haida built water-tight boxes for cooking salmon and other fish. Women filled the boxes with water and added hot rocks from the fire, one at a time, until the water came to a boil. They then cooked the fish in the boiling water.

Many Haida people were expert carvers. They created designs on boxes, masks, tools, and totem poles. Ravens, bears, beavers, eagles, and other animals or symbols decorated Haidas' towering totem poles. For the Haida people, certain animals held religious significance. Totem poles also represented family histories or honored a deceased relative.

Potlatches

Many American Indian tribes of the Northwest held potlatches. These celebrations of feasting and gift-giving often honored the birth of a child or a marriage. Early tribes prepared potlatches after a successful whale hunt or when salmon was abundant. At these times, a chief invited neighboring tribes to share the large meal. During potlatch celebrations, hosts presented valuable gifts to the guests of honor.

Grilled Salmon
with Blackberries and Green Onions

Ingredients
3 salmon steaks, 1-inch
(2.5 centimeters) thick,
about 6 ounces each
1 bunch green onions
3 tablespoons olive oil
¼ cup fresh or
frozen blackberries

Equipment
paper towel
plate
cutting board
sharp knife
measuring spoons
2 small bowls
dry-ingredient
measuring cups
pastry brush
tongs

1. Heat grill or broiler.
2. Rinse salmon steaks and pat dry with paper towel. Set on plate.
3. Cut roots off bulb end of onions and trim top 3 inches (8 centimeters) of onion greens.
4. Measure 3 tablespoons olive oil into a small bowl. Put ¼ cup blackberries into another small bowl.
5. Arrange whole onions on grill or broiler pan. Brush with olive oil. Grill or broil about 1 minute. Turn with tongs. Grill or broil another minute. Move onions to side of grill or broiler pan.
6. Brush both sides of the salmon steaks with olive oil.

7. Place steaks on grill or broiler pan. Cook for 3 to 5 minutes. Turn salmon and brush with olive oil again. Grill or broil another 3 to 5 minutes. Salmon is done when flesh whitens slightly and flakes when pressed with a fork.
8. Before removing steaks from grill or broiler, put a spoonful of blackberries on top of each steak. Cook 1 minute longer.
9. Remove steaks from grill onto serving plates. Arrange a few green onions on top of each steak and serve immediately.

Makes 3 servings

*Haida carved
designs into
hunting tools.*

California: Acorns, a Chumash Meal

The Chumash Indians lived along the coast of what is now California. The region's warm climate and coastal waters offered the Chumash a wide variety of foods. They fished along the Pacific coast and gathered berries, greens, cattails, and roots from surrounding forests and grasslands. They also collected eggs from the nests of migratory birds that settled in coves. The Chumash ate eggs raw or boiled.

The Chumash based their diet on foods from the sea. They could depend on a constant supply of numerous species of fish. Along the shoreline, they also gathered mussels, clams, and abalone, a mollusk similar to a snail. Chumash hunters traveled inland to hunt a variety of animals. In the forests and prairies, they hunted squirrels, rabbits, and prairie dogs. They hunted deer, elk, and bears with blowguns, snares, and bows and arrows.

Acorns were an important food in the Chumash diet. The Chumash often ate breads and puddings made from acorn meal with fish and meat. To make acorn meal, Chumash women collected, dried, and shelled acorns. They then ground the nuts into a fine powder between two stones. This powder contained a bitter chemical called tannin. Chumash women leached the tannin out of the meal by rinsing it with water. They dug pits in sand and poured water over the meal until the tannin washed out.

Women boiled meat, fish, and acorn mush in tightly woven baskets. These baskets were watertight. At every meal, Chumash families ate acorn mush, a hot pudding made from acorn meal. Chumash women mixed acorn meal with water in the baskets and placed hot rocks in the mixture. The meal thickened as it cooked.

Chumash men fished for swordfish, tuna, halibut, and sardines in long, narrow boats called tomols. To catch fish, hunters used nets, harpoons, and hooks made of mussel and abalone shells.

14

Acorn Cakes

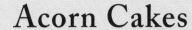

Ingredients

½ cup pine nuts
¾ cup acorn meal or acorn flour
  (available in most Korean markets and
  many health food stores)
¼ cup all-purpose flour
1 teaspoon baking powder
1 teaspoon salt
½ cup water
1 egg
2 tablespoons vegetable oil
2 tablespoons honey
3 tablespoons additional vegetable oil
small jar of honey for serving

Equipment

baking pan, 9 inches by 13 inches
  (23 centimeters by 33 centimeters)
pot holders
small mixing bowl
dry-ingredient measuring cups
measuring spoons
liquid measuring cup
wooden spoon
large skillet
metal spatula
serving platter or large plate

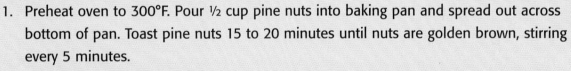

1. Preheat oven to 300°F. Pour ½ cup pine nuts into baking pan and spread out across bottom of pan. Toast pine nuts 15 to 20 minutes until nuts are golden brown, stirring every 5 minutes.

2. In small mixing bowl, combine ¾ cup acorn meal or flour, ¼ cup flour, 1 teaspoon baking powder, and 1 teaspoon salt. Add ½ cup water, 1 egg, 2 tablespoons vegetable oil, and 2 tablespoons honey. Mix until flour is completely moistened. Stir in pine nuts.

3. Heat 1 tablespoon vegetable oil in large skillet over medium heat.

4. Pour ¼ cup acorn batter into hot skillet. After 30 seconds, flip cakes with a metal spatula. Cook about 1 minute. Watch carefully. Cakes cook quickly. Remove cake to serving platter or plate.

5. Repeat step 4 with remaining batter, adding 1 tablespoon oil after every three cakes.

6. Serve immediately and top each serving with honey.

Makes 8 acorn cakes

The Southwest: Hopi Farmers

The Hopi and many other American Indian groups of the Southwest built their villages on high, flat buttes called mesas. The steep-sided mesas offered the tribes many advantages. They could more easily watch for enemies and guard their villages against attack. They also could keep watch over their crops, which were planted below in the valleys.

The Hopi people, like most southwestern American Indians, depended on farming to give them a steady supply of food. They grew squash, beans, and various colors of corn. Blue corn, which grew well in the dry climate, was their most important crop. The small amount of rain that the desert area received drained down the mesa to water the fields. The Hopi dug holes for corn seeds about 15 to 18 inches (38 to 46 centimeters) deep. The deep holes kept the plants' roots in damp sand. Workers planted the corn seeds 10 to 15 inches (25 to 38 centimeters) apart to make sure each plant could take enough water from the ground.

Hopi women made flat bread called piki from blue or red corn. They mixed ground blue corn with finely sifted ashes and spring water until the dough was thick and smooth. Piki bread was crêpe-like, baked with one, thin layer of batter. Taking a small handful at a time, Hopi women spread the mixture across a flat, heated stone. Each piki cooked quickly and was folded into a packet shape. The Hopi served platters of rolled piki bread at religious celebrations, festivals, and special events. Piki smelled and tasted like cornbread.

Some American Indians of the southwest used baking ovens built with a mixture of clay and grass called adobe.

Hopi women made piki bread for celebrations and ceremonies.

Hopi, like many American Indians before 1500, ground dried corn into meal by crushing it with a stone.

The Hopi planted vegetables in personal dry gardens on the mesas. These gardens received water only when it rained. Carrying water up steep cliffs to the mesas was difficult, so the Hopi reserved this water for cooking and drinking. Hopi gardens produced mainly squash and beans. Hopi grew many tepary beans, which thrived in the low moisture and high temperatures of the Southwest. The Hopi boiled or baked tepary beans or ground them into meal.

Hopi women also gathered wild foods from the surrounding desert. They picked cactus buds, prickly pear fruit, sunflower seeds, and grass seeds. Yucca, a lilylike flower, was a useful plant for many tribes of the Southwest. Yucca leaves could be peeled into thin needles to use for sewing. The Hopi also used yucca roots as soap. Yucca fruits were a delicious treat.

Cooking Utensils

American Indians made cooking and eating utensils from wood, bark, pottery, shells, animal bones, skins, and dried vegetable skins. They carved spoons and ladles from goat and buffalo horns and wood. American Indians saved squash and gourd skins and dried them to use as bowls. Many American Indian groups cut elaborate carvings into wooden bowls and spoons. They sometimes tied seashells to the ends of wooden sticks for scooping soups or beverages.

American Indians of the Pacific Northwest made this goat horn spoon and carved dish.

Squash Stew

Ingredients

2 butternut squash, about
  1 ½ pounds each
1 small onion
1 cup fresh corn kernels or
  thawed frozen corn
1 can (16 ounces) cooked
  pinto beans, undrained
½ teaspoon ground cumin
½ teaspoon salt
¼ teaspoon pepper
½ cup chopped parsley
1 tablespoon butter or
  margarine for greasing

Equipment

can opener
cutting board
large, sharp knife
spoon
small, sharp knife
small bowl
medium mixing bowl
dry-ingredient measuring
  cups
measuring spoons
baking pan, 9 inches by
  13 inches (23 centimeters
  by 33 centimeters)
aluminum foil
pot holders
paper towel or napkin
baking sheet

1. Preheat oven to 350°F.
2. Cut each squash in half lengthwise with large knife. Scoop out seeds and set aside. Rinse squash well.
3. Hollow out the inside of each squash half by cutting the squash meat out of the neck and bottom. Leave a ¾-inch (2-centimeter) edge all the way around. Place the removed squash pieces on cutting board.
4. Chop squash chunks into small pieces and put in small bowl. Set aside.
5. Cut ends off the onion. Peel off outer papery layer. Cut onion into ½-inch (1.3-centimeter) slices. Chop slices into small pieces.
6. Place onion in medium mixing bowl. Add 1 cup corn, 1 can pinto beans and liquid, ½ teaspoon cumin, ½ teaspoon salt, ¼ teaspoon pepper, and ½ cup parsley. Stir well.
7. Stir squash pieces into corn and bean mixture.
8. Place squash skins in baking pan. Scoop corn, bean, and squash mixture into the hollowed-out squash skins.
9. Cover each squash with aluminum foil. Bake for 1 hour to 1 hour and 15 minutes, or until squash is tender. Serve immediately.
10. Rinse seeds in wire mesh strainer.
11. Use paper towel or napkin dabbed with 1 tablespoon butter or margarine to lightly grease baking sheet.
12. Spread seeds over baking sheet. Roast during the last 15 minutes while squash bakes. Serve with stew.

Makes 4 to 6 servings

Great Basin: The Nomadic Shoshone

Finding large amounts of food in the Great Basin region was a challenge for the Shoshone people. Little rainfall made the land too dry to plant and harvest crops. American Indians living in the Great Basin region did not have enough food to support large villages. They traveled in small nomadic groups, or bands, moving with the seasons or to find food.

The Shoshone people lived in temporary shelters made from sticks, branches, and brush. They searched the surrounding area for chokecherries and serviceberries. They also dug for many edible roots and gathered seeds and bulbs from plants. In the fall, the Shoshone gathered pine nuts and sunflower seeds. They roasted the seeds and added them to soups. The Shoshone also found wild onion roots to flavor soup and meat.

The Shoshone often gathered cattails. In early spring, the Shoshone picked cattail shoots to peel and cook or to eat raw. The young flower heads of cattails were boiled and eaten like corn on the cob or a pickle. During the summer, the Shoshone shook cattail flower heads to loosen the pollen and collected it in pouches. They mixed the high-protein pollen with other grains and seeds. Shoshone dried cattail roots and ground them into meal.

Shoshone hunters did not carry heavy weapons for hunting large animals. Aside from an occasional deer or antelope, they mainly hunted rabbits, squirrels, prairie dogs, and grouse. A swarm of grasshoppers, herded into pits lined with hot coals, was roasted to make a meal. The Shoshone also roasted and dried crickets, ants, and cicadas.

American Indians dug for turnips, sunchokes, and other edible roots with digging sticks.

Roasted Seed Soup

Ingredients

1 cup toasted pine nuts
4 green onions
1 medium carrot or parsnip
5 cups water
2 small vegetable broth cubes
1 1/2 cups salted sunflower nuts

Equipment

baking pan, 9 inches by 13 inches
   (23 centimeters by 33 centimeters)
pot holders
dry-ingredient measuring cups
cutting board
sharp knife
2 small bowls
large saucepan
liquid measuring cup
wooden spoon

1. Preheat oven to 300°F.
2. Spread 1 cup pine nuts across the bottom of baking pan. Toast pine nuts for 15 to 20 minutes until nuts are golden brown, stirring every 5 minutes.
3. Turn oven off when finished.
4. Cut off top roots and green stems of onions. Chop onion into 1/4-inch (.6-centimeter) slices. Put chopped onion into a small bowl and set aside.
5. Slice carrot or parsnip into 1/2-inch (1.3-centimeter) pieces. Put in small bowl and set aside.
6. In large saucepan, combine 5 cups water and 2 broth cubes. Bring to a boil. Continue boiling until broth cubes completely dissolve.
7. Stir in carrots and green onions. Return to boiling. Lower heat and cook over medium heat about 10 minutes, or until carrot is tender. Stir in 1 1/2 cups sunflower nuts and 1 cup toasted pine nuts. Lower heat to simmer. Cook another 20 minutes.

Makes about 8 servings

21

The Hidatsa tribe lived on the Great Plains in the area that became the state of North Dakota. Hidatsa women constructed dome-shaped earth lodges from timber, willows, slough grass, and sod. A large earth lodge could measure more than 40 feet (12 meters) across. In the center of the lodge, Hidatsa women left an open hole in the roof. This opening allowed light to enter the lodge and smoke from the fire to drift out. Hidatsa families built villages of earth lodges on bluffs along the Missouri River. They lived in these lodges throughout the spring and summer months.

During the fall and winter months, Hidatsa built smaller earth lodges in wooded areas near the Missouri River. These winter homes sometimes had an attached tunnel that led to a twin lodge. This small addition housed the sick or elderly or became a playhouse for the children. Hidatsa families returned to their permanent villages in the spring.

Hidatsa women were expert gardeners. Grandmothers often taught valuable gardening skills to their granddaughters. In spring, each family planted fields of corn and gardens of squash and beans. Women dried and stored much of the fall harvest to last throughout the long, bitter-cold winters.

Women made mapee nakapah (mah-PEE nah-kah-PAH) from squash, beans, and corn. They cut a string of dried squash and tied the ends together. They then boiled the ring of squash with a couple handfuls of beans in a pot. Meanwhile, they parched some corn in a clay pot and roasted sticks of buffalo fat over the fire. After the squash and beans had softened, Hidatsa cooks removed the ring and mashed the squash in a wooden bowl. They then pounded the parched corn and fat in a mortar. The cornmeal and squash were added to the pot of beans for a filling meal.

American Indians fashioned tools from animal bones and wood. The blade of this garden hoe was made from a buffalo shoulder bone.

Hidatsa Corn-watchers' Stages

Hidatsa people believed that corn plants had souls. The Hidatsa protected and cared for growing corn so that none of it went to waste. In the cornfields, Hidatsas built tall platforms called watchers' stages. Watchers' stages were about 4 feet by 3 feet (1.2 meters by .9 meters) wide, large enough to comfortably fit two girls. Gardeners often left a tree standing in the field to shade the stage. Hidatsa girls began corn watching when they were 10 to 12 years old.

From the watchers' stage, girls sang songs to the corn and scared away pesky birds by waving blankets and shaking rattles. The girls chased away an occasional boy who tried to sneak an ear of sweet, green corn. Older women sometimes climbed onto the stage and sang songs while they took a rest from their gardening.

Most American Indian tribes harvested corn. They roasted some ears of corn when the corn ripened. American Indians let other ears of corn dry out. Dried corn was ground into meal for making bread and pudding.

During summer, women gathered wild Juneberries and chokecherries and dug up wild turnips. Hidatsa women sometimes pounded the turnips into meal and added dried Juneberries to make a sweet pudding.

Between planting and harvesting, a group of men and women left the village for several weeks for the buffalo hunt. After a kill, the women helped the men cut the meat into strips to dry. They roasted some of the meat to eat fresh. In the evenings, members of the hunt often sat around the fire and exchanged stories.

Hidatsa often ate buffalo meat for breakfast. They boiled the meat in water to soften it. The broth from the meat served as a hot tea. The Hidatsa drank the broth mainly in the winter months when it warmed a cold stomach.

Hidatsa considered it polite to serve food when visitors stopped by the earth lodge. Hosts gave visiting friends and family a bowl of food when they arrived. If the guests could not finish their food, they took the leftovers home.

A Hidatsa earth lodge had a sturdy, timber frame. Women prepared food on tables inside the lodge.

Pemmican

Ingredients

1 package (4-ounces)
  beef jerky
1 cup mixed golden
  raisins and dried
  cherries or other
  dried fruit mixture
3 tablespoons melted
butter
1 tablespoon butter for greasing

Equipment

dry-ingredient measuring cups
small bowl
food processor
small, microwaveable dish
paper towel
baking pan, 8 inches by 8 inches
  (20 centimeters by 20 centimeters)
rubber spatula
aluminum foil
sharp knife

1. Mix 1 cup dried fruit together in small bowl.
2. In food processor, process jerky until it is in small pieces.
3. Add dried fruit to food processor. Process until fruit is cut into smaller pieces and is well mixed with jerky.
4. In a small, microwaveable dish, melt 3 tablespoons butter.
5. Add melted butter. Process several short pulses until well mixed.
6. Use paper towel dabbed with 1 tablespoon butter to lightly grease baking pan.
7. Using rubber spatula, press pemmican into a thin layer in pan. Cover with aluminum foil and refrigerate.
8. When chilled, cut into small squares.

Makes about 64 pieces of pemmican

The Iroquois were farmers and hunters who lived in the Northeast. American Indians of the Northeast had a short growing season. Many groups grew gardens full of corn, beans, pumpkins, and squash. These vegetables could be dried and stored for winter use. The Iroquois stored dried foods in the ground or hung them from frame posts in their houses. Women soaked bean and squash seeds in water prior to planting to make the plants grow more quickly.

The Iroquois built longhouses in permanent villages. These narrow houses could be up to 150 feet (46 meters) long. Longhouse frames were covered with sheets of elm bark. Longhouses had a door on either end and a row of smokeholes down the center of the roof.

In the spring, Iroquois families gathered wild strawberries and Juneberries. They also picked plums, grapes, cherries, and crab apples.

Corn was an important vegetable for the Iroquois. Ears of corn were dried in cribs. These small storage

American Indians who lived along the shores of the Great Lakes harvested wild rice.

buildings had open slats along the sides that allowed air to move through the corn to keep it from rotting. Iroquois women roasted corn kernels to make parched corn, which also stored well.

Iroquois women baked cornmeal into puddings and breads, which they sweetened with maple syrup or dried berries. Iroquois families also ate succotash, a thick vegetable dish made with hominy and beans.

Corn husks served as baking dishes for cakes and breads. Women wrapped cornmeal cakes in the leaves and set them on hot ashes.

Iroquois hunted wild game with bows and arrows or set traps to catch the animals. Deer meat, or venison, was the main meat of the Iroquois. Men also hunted elk, bear, moose, and beaver. Iroquois families were especially fond of roasted beaver tail. Iroquois hunters searched for ducks, geese, wild turkeys, and passenger pigeons. They fished the coastal waters and rivers with nets for trout, bass, perch, whitefish, and eels.

Maple-glazed Turkey Legs and Baked Wild Rice

Ingredients

1 ½ cups water
4 chicken bouillon cubes
1 medium onion
1 cup wild rice
1 tablespoon butter or
  margarine for greasing
3 turkey legs
⅓ cup maple syrup

Equipment

glass liquid measuring cup
pot holder
spoon
cutting board
sharp knife
2 small bowls
dry-ingredient measuring cup
fine-mesh strainer

baking pan, 9 inches by
  13 inches (23 centimeters
  by 33 centimeters)
paper towel or napkin
wooden spoon
pastry brush
aluminum foil or baking pan
tongs

1. Fill glass liquid measuring cup with 1 ½ cups water. Add 4 bouillon cubes. Microwave on HIGH about 4 to 5 minutes.

2. Remove from microwave oven with a pot holder. Stir to dissolve bouillon cubes.

3. Cut both ends off onion. Peel off outer papery layer and cut into ½-inch (1.3-centimeter) slices. Chop slices into small pieces. Put chopped onion into small bowl.

4. Rinse 1 cup wild rice in fine-mesh strainer under running water.

5. Use paper towel dabbed with 1 tablespoon butter or margarine to lightly grease baking pan.

6. Carefully pour bouillon water into baking pan. Gently stir in onion and wild rice. Set aside.

7. Turn on oven broiler.

8. Pour ⅓ cup maple syrup into the other small bowl.

9. Place turkey legs on a plate. Brush maple syrup over turkey legs using the pastry brush.

10. Line broiler with a sheet of aluminum foil. If your broiler is not a separate compartment, place turkey legs in another baking pan and place directly into the oven. Broil for 3 minutes.

11. Use tongs and pot holders to flip the turkey legs. Brush the other side of legs with maple syrup. Broil another 3 minutes.

12. With tongs, remove legs from aluminum foil or baking pan and place on top of rice mixture.

13. Reduce oven to 300°F. Cover baking pan with aluminum foil. Bake about 1 to 1 ½ hours, brushing turkey legs with maple syrup every 20 minutes. Bake until turkey legs are cooked through and rice is tender.

Makes 6 servings

The Cherokee people lived in large villages in southeastern North America. Each village consisted of 30 to 60 houses that surrounded a large meeting building. Each dome-shaped house had a wattle frame, which was made from woven twigs and branches. Cherokee covered the wattle frame with a mud or clay paste called daub.

Cherokee ate both garden foods and wild plants. Corn, beans, squash, and wild yams grew in the Cherokees' large gardens. Women collected raspberries, strawberries, cranberries, blackberries, and gooseberries. They also searched for grapes, mulberries, and wild cherries. These fruits could be dried to add to breads and puddings during winter months. Cherokee dug for wild onions and ground nuts and picked wild greens and mushrooms.

Cherokee also dug for sunchokes. These tuber vegetables resemble a potato or ginger roots and are crisp and somewhat sweet. Cherokee added raw, sliced sunchokes to salads or roasted them as a side dish.

Cherokee groups built their villages near rivers and streams. They fished these waters with spears and nets. Along the coast, Cherokee caught sturgeon, herring, and turtles with fishhooks made from bone. On beaches, they collected oysters, mussels, and clams.

Wild game was plentiful in the eastern woodlands. Cherokee hunted deer, rabbits, squirrels, bears, beaver, otter, turkey, ducks, geese, and pigeons with bows and arrows. Some tribes set traps for animals. Women prepared meals over hot coals on an open fire. Many foods were layered with seaweed or wet leaves and steamed. Cherokee families ate mainly soups and stews, which they served in a single pot.

Cherokee searched their land for spices and natural sweetners to flavor foods. To sweeten breads and puddings, Cherokee collected spicebush berries and honey. Cherokee gathered wild crab apples from forests and baked them over an open fire for a treat.

Garden Pan Bread

Ingredients
1 cup cornmeal
1 cup all-purpose flour
2 teaspoons baking powder
½ teaspoon salt
¾ cup mashed pumpkin
1 cup water
2 eggs
½ cup raisins
½ cup chopped walnuts
1 tablespoon butter for greasing

Equipment
medium bowl
dry-ingredient measuring cups
measuring spoons
wooden spoon
small bowl
liquid measuring cup
paper towel or napkin
9-inch (23-centimeter) cast-iron skillet or
 baking pan, 9 inches by 9 inches
 (23 centimeters by 23 centimeters)
pot holders

1. Preheat oven to 350°F.
2. In medium bowl, combine 1 cup cornmeal, 1 cup flour, 2 teaspoons baking powder, and ½ teaspoon salt. Set aside.
3. In a small bowl, combine ¾ cup pumpkin, 1 cup water, and 2 eggs. Stir until well-mixed.
4. Stir pumpkin mixture into cornmeal mixture. Mix until dry ingredients are moistened. Gently stir in ½ cup raisins and ½ cup walnuts.
5. Use a paper towel or napkin dabbed with 1 tablespoon butter or margarine to grease skillet or baking pan.
6. Spoon batter into skillet or baking pan.
7. Bake for 30 to 35 minutes or until bread is golden brown and pulls away from edges. A wooden toothpick inserted into the center of the bread will come out clean.

Makes 8 to 9 servings

Cherokee, Iroquois, and other eastern groups gathered hickory nuts, walnuts, and pecans from surrounding forests. They ground seeds, nuts, and corn into meal with a hollowed out log, called a mortar, and a heavy stick.

Words to Know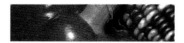

archeologist (ar-kee-OL-uh-jist)—a scientist who studies the material remains of past human life

bands (BANDS)—groups of people that live and move together

cattail (KAT-tayl)—a plant that has tall, thin stalks with furry, brown pods at the top of each stalk; cattails grow in wet, marshy areas.

crib (KRIB)—a small farm building with slatted sides used for drying corn

earth lodge (URTH LOJ)—a dome-shaped house constructed of sod, bark, and mud

edible (ED-uh-buhl)—can be eaten

eulachon (yoo-luh-KAHN)—an oily fish related to smelt, sometimes called candlefish

mattak (mat-TAK)—a layer of whale fat

mesa (MAY-suh)—a tall butte or hill that has steep sides and a flat top; explorers of the Southwest named these hills mesas, which is the Spanish word for table.

nomadic (noh-MA-dik)—traveling from area to area rather than living in the same place

tomols (toh-MAWLS)—an 8-foot to 30-foot (2.5-meter to 9-meter) canoe made of redwood or driftwood

totem pole (TOH-tuhm POHL)—a tall, wooden pole carved with animals, plants, or other symbols that represent a family or group

To Learn More

Bial, Raymond. *The Iroquois*. Lifeways. New York: Benchmark Books, 1999.

Kavasch, E. Barrie. *Native Harvests: American Indian Wild Foods and Recipes*. Washington, Conn.: Birdstone Books, 1998.

Lassieur, Allison. *The Inuit*. Native Peoples. Mankato, Minn.: Bridgestone Books, 2000.

Long, Cathryn. *The Cherokee*. Indigenous People of North America. San Diego: Lucent Books, 2000.

Moss, Nathaniel. *The Shoshone Indians*. The Junior Library of American Indians. Broomall, Pa.: Chelsea Juniors, 1997.

Waheenee. *Waheenee, an Indian Girl's Story*. Lincoln: University of Nebraska Press, 1981.

Yue, Charlotte and David Yue. *The Wigwam and the Longhouse*. Boston, Mass.: Houghton Mifflin, 2000.

Places to Write and Visit

Cahokia Mounds State Historic Site
30 Ramey Street
Collinsville, IL 62234

Canadian Museum of Civilization
100 Laurier Street
Station 8
Hull, Quebec J8X 4H2
Canada

**Knife River Indian Village
 National Historic Site**
P.O. Box 9
Stanton, ND 58571

The National Museum of the American Indian
The George Gustav Heye Center
Alexander Hamilton U.S. Custom House
One Bowling Green
New York, NY 10004

Internet Sites

Cahokia Mounds
http://www.cahokiamounds.com

Canadian Museum of Civilization
http://www.civilization.ca/cmc/cmceng/welcmeng.html

The First Americans
http://www.germantown.k12.il.us/html/intro.html

The Institute for American Indian Studies
http://www.amerindianinstitute.org

Inuit Games
http://www.ahs.uwaterloo.ca/~museum/vexhibit/
inuit/english/inuit.html

**The Santa Barbara Museum of Natural History:
Chumash Life**
http://www.sbnature.org/chumash/intro.htm

Index